Consumer *Spending*

The Wise Buyer | Shopping for Goods

Shopping for Services | Consumer Rights

LIFE SKILLS

HANDBOOKS

Car and Driver

Community Resources and Safety

Consumer Spending

Everyday Household Tasks

Getting Ahead at Work

Health and Wellness

Managing Money

Moving Out on Your Own

Transportation

Workplace Readiness

SADDLEBACK
EDUCATIONAL PUBLISHING
www.sdlback.com

ISBN: 978-1-68021-983-8
eBook: 978-1-64598-781-9

Printed in Malaysia
26 25 24 23 22   1 2 3 4 5

TABLE OF CONTENTS

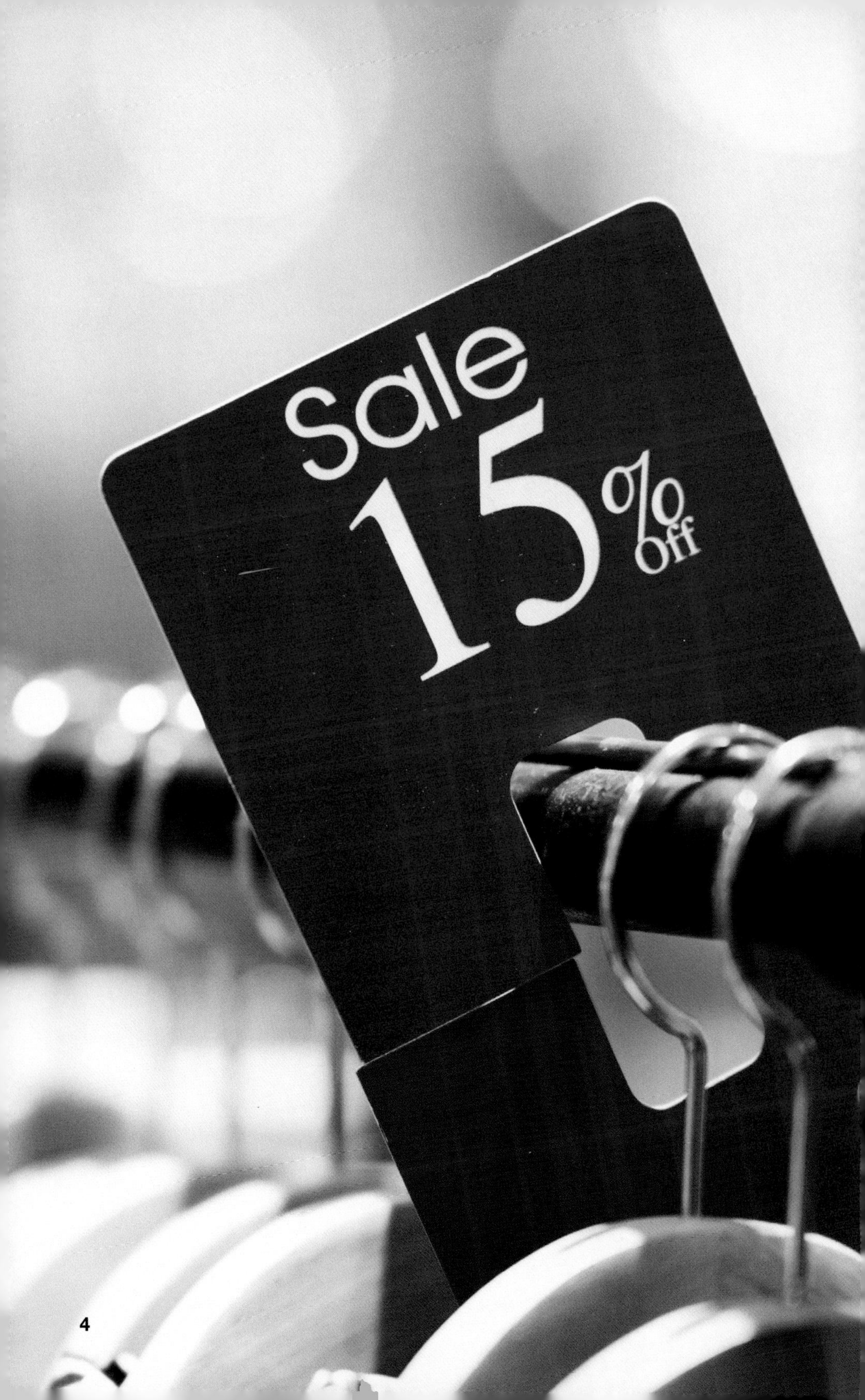
Sale
15%
off

The Wise Buyer

Everyone loves finding a great deal while shopping. It's thrilling to get a top-quality item for a low price. How do you know the true quality of an item though? Is there a way to tell if you're really getting a good price? Understanding some basic principles of smart shopping can help you answer these questions. Learning about advertising, estimates, and bargain hunting is a smart idea too. This will help you avoid getting taken advantage of.

The Smartest Shopper

Lynne often met her friends at the mall on Saturdays. They had fun shopping.

One friend, Kacie, loved fashion. She enjoyed reading fashion magazines and watching fashion shows on TV. Then she'd tell her friends about the latest styles. But Kacie didn't know much about the quality of clothes. Shopping around or waiting for items to go on sale wasn't her style. Instead, she bought what she wanted, when she wanted. It didn't matter if she paid full price.

Another friend, Grace, claimed to be a bargain hunter. She knew about all the stores that sold clothes for reduced prices. Sometimes she shopped for used clothes at a local thrift store. But the bargains Grace found could have issues with quality and fit. Once, she found some jeans for a really low price. The first time she wore them, the zipper broke. A few weeks later, she bought a coat that was too big just because it was on sale.

The smartest shopper in the group was Lynne. Before making a purchase, she looked around at several stores. She also checked prices and watched for sales. Buying quality items was important to her too. Lynne didn't buy everything she wanted. But what she bought was well-made and looked good on her. When Lynne bought a new outfit, it had to be something she could wear many times.

Chapter 1
Principles of Smart Shopping

Are you a smart shopper?
Learning how to make wise
buying decisions will save
you money and increase your
satisfaction with purchases.
Follow these simple steps:

1. **Learn about a product before you buy it.** Read the product's
   label. Find out what's inside the package. Also ask people who
   own the same product or something similar for their opinions.
   Would they recommend the product? Do they have any
   complaints about it? Ask where they purchased the product.
   Did they get a good buy?

   Newspaper, magazine, and online ads can give you facts
   about different brands. Reviews can too. Compare the prices
   of products using ads. Read articles and customer reviews to
   learn more about how products perform. Consumer Reports
   offers some free product reviews. With a paid subscription, the
   organization provides access to more comprehensive reviews.
   These reports test and grade products. Reading the reviews will
   help you learn which products you can trust to last.

2. **Compare what you learn about different brands.** List the advantages and disadvantages of each. This will help you compare different products. For example, Tom is looking for a lightweight, waterproof watch. He's a lifeguard and needs a watch he can count on. First, he researches a few brands. Then, he lists advantages and disadvantages for each one. This list helps Tom compare features of several watches.

3. **Consider your wants and needs.** These are as important as the price you pay for something. Tom decides to buy a watch that has fewer features. Still, it costs more than many others because it's waterproof. Being waterproof is a key feature he needs for his work.

Where to Shop

Where you shop can make a big difference in how much you pay. Discount stores and buyer warehouses usually offer the lowest prices. But be sure you know what you want and how much it costs before you shop at one of these stores. They may sell a mix of high- and low-quality brands. Customer service or advice may be limited. You often can't try on clothes at these stores either.

Retail and specialty stores charge the highest prices. But they usually sell top-quality brands. Their customer service is good too. If you shop at a retail store, ask about upcoming sales. You can save a lot by waiting until prices drop.

When to Shop

When you go shopping is important too. Don't rush out to buy a new type of product the minute it's introduced. Wait several months. By then, the price will have likely gone down. It often pays to wait.

Prices change on seasonal items too. For instance, you'll pay less for a swimsuit at the end of summer than at the beginning. You'll save money on a space heater if you buy it in the summer, not the winter.

Smart shoppers also wait for sales that occur around major holidays. For example, after the winter holidays, you can often find decorations on sale. Gift wrap items will also be discounted. Consider stocking up for the next year. Keep an eye out for newspaper or TV ads and mailers to learn about these sales.

When Can You Get the Best Deals?

Products used during certain times of the year cost less in the off-season. Others go on sale during particular months. Can you wait to buy something you want or need? If you can, you'll likely save money. Here's when you'll find good deals on popular items:

January

- Bedding and linens
- Computers
- Exercise equipment

February

- TVs
- Electronics

March

- Cell phones
- Digital cameras

April

- Spring clothing
- Lawn mowers
- Vacuums

May

- Athletic wear
- Camping gear
- Mattresses

June

- Indoor furniture
- Summer sports gear
- Dishes and cookware

July

- Furniture
- Swimwear

August

- Air conditioners
- School supplies
- Outdoor furniture

September

- Bikes
- Cars

October

- Toys
- Wedding supplies

November

- Baby products
- GPS systems
- Recreational vehicles

December

- Home appliances
- Tools

Chapter 2

Interpreting Ad Copy

Advertisements, or ads, try to convince you to buy or do things. First, ad writers try to get your attention:

Then, they try to convince you that you're getting a deal:

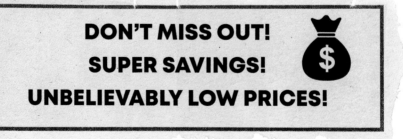

Facts Versus Opinions

Knowing the differences between facts and opinions is important. This is true even for shopping. If an ad says, "All items now on sale for half price," that's a fact. You could go into the store and prove that to be true or false. Facts are things that can be proven.

"Unbelievably low prices" isn't a fact. It's an opinion. Opinions are ideas or beliefs. Some people may agree with them. Others may not.

Ways to Advertise

- **Online:** Ads placed on websites and social media sites
- **Direct mail:** Letters and postcards sent in the mail
- **Print:** Newspapers and magazines
- **Signs:** Billboards and signs on buses and taxis
- **Television and movies:** Commercials and products used in shows
- **Radio:** Commercials and products mentioned in programs
- **Word of mouth:** People talking about the product

Can you tell the difference between facts and opinions? Read the six ads below. Which are facts, and which are opinions?

1. Deal of a Lifetime!

2. All Items on Sale Through May 31

3. Nothing Over $10.00

4. Shoes Priced for Every Budget

5. Best Prices Anywhere!

6. Portable Bluetooth Speaker—Only $49.99

Answers: 1. Opinion, 2. Fact, 3. Fact, 4. Opinion, 5. Opinion, 6. Fact

Why is it important to interpret ads correctly? Knowing how to read ads can help you compare prices and locate the best buys. Ads can help you find a service you might need. They may also tell you about special sales or new products.

How Do Ads Convince You?

Ads use many methods to try to convince you to do something. Here are some of the most common:

- **Misleading words:** Ad writers use words such as *new, fresh, natural, improved,* and *healthy* to make their products sound good. But don't be fooled. Look for facts to help you decide if the words are being used truthfully.

- **Comparatives:** Nearly all ads use comparatives. These are words that compare things. Comparatives usually end in -er, such as *brighter, faster, or smoother.* When you hear a comparative being used, ask yourself what the product is being compared to (e.g., "Brighter than what?"). If the ad doesn't say, then it's simply stating an opinion.

Truth in Advertising

In the United States, there are laws protecting consumers from false or misleading ads. Advertisers must have proof that their claims are true and fair. If you become a victim of false advertising, you can file a complaint. This is your right. The Federal Trade Commission (FTC) enforces advertising laws. To file a complaint, go online to the FTC's website.

- **Exaggerations:** Ad writers tend to exaggerate. They often say things are bigger, better, cheaper, or more important than they really are. Exaggerations get your attention and make you want to act right away. Here's an example:

EVERY MORNING, THE PEOPLE IN YOUR TOWN WAKE UP TO BILLIONS OF BITS OF DUST AND OTHER ALLERGY-CAUSING MATERIALS.

PROTECT YOURSELF NOW! ALLERGY-FREE IS ON THE JOB!

Ask questions if you think an ad exaggerates. Are there really billions of bits of dust? Do they really bother people? Is this a problem you need to solve? The ad doesn't say.

More Ways That Ads Convince You

- **Snob appeal:** A product is connected with being wealthy or famous.

- **Cause and effect:** Using a product will solve a problem or make your troubles go away.

- **Testimonial:** Someone talks about the benefits of the product based on his or her personal experience with it.

- **Bandwagon:** Peer pressure is used to convince buyers that everyone wants a particular product.

- **Plain folks:** A product is connected with everyday people or common experiences.

- **Emotional appeal:** A product is linked with emotions, such as fear or happiness.

Chapter 3

Avoiding Unexpected Costs

Kayla bought a new showerhead and faucet for her bathtub. Then she called a plumber to install these new fixtures. The plumber gave her a written estimate. It stated that the job would cost about $160 in labor.

After agreeing to the price, Kayla signed the estimate. This **authorized** the plumber to do the work.

The plumber installed the fixtures. Then he gave Kayla a bill for $479.50. The amount shocked her. It was nearly three times the estimated cost.

What Went Wrong?

Kayla did not carefully read the paper she signed. By signing it, she authorized the plumber to do any extra work he felt was needed.

The plumber looked at Kayla's old pipes. He didn't think they would fit her new bathroom fixtures. To replace them, he charged her extra. In the process, the plumber removed some tiles around the bathtub. Replacing them also went on Kayla's bill.

Kayla didn't think the extra work was needed. But she still had to pay the bill. There was nothing she could do about it.

How Can You Protect Yourself?

Has a similar situation ever happened to you? Can you think of ways to avoid such expensive surprises? Follow these tips:

- Always get more than one estimate for a job. Repair people usually give estimates for free. If they want to charge you for an estimate, don't use them. Kayla should have asked at least one other plumber for an estimate. Another plumber might have warned her about matching new fixtures to old pipes.

- Make sure you understand what you're signing. Read all agreements carefully. You might want to make changes. Now is the time to do so. Once you've signed a **contract**, you've authorized the work to be done. Kayla signed too soon. Then changes could not be made. She could have written a **clause** into the plumbing estimate. It may have said, "Further authorization needed if charges will be more than $250."

- If any parts were replaced, ask to see the old parts. Then you can see why they were removed. Kayla should have asked to see the old pipes. The plumber could have shown how they didn't work with her new fixtures.

- Find out whether the repairs were done with new or rebuilt parts. Some things can be repaired with used parts that have been fixed up or redone. Rebuilt parts are cheaper than new parts. Some are just as good too. Ask about using rebuilt parts ahead of time. Also be sure to check the bill you get after the work is done. If the repair service said rebuilt parts were used, make sure you don't pay for new parts. The reverse is true too. If you're charged for new parts, be sure that rebuilt parts were not installed.

- Be on the lookout for **fraud**. Take questionable decisions and actions seriously. Report any repair person or service provider that cheats you. Your state's **consumer protection agency** may be able to help you get your money back. You'll need to have copies of your estimate and bill to prove you were cheated.

Tips for Finding Good Repair People

- Ask people you know what repair companies they use. Talk to your friends, neighbors, coworkers, and family members.

- Interview and get estimates from at least three service providers. Do this even for small jobs.

- Find out if any complaints have been filed against the repair companies you're considering. Check with your state's consumer protection agency.

- For each repair person, get the contact information of at least three previous customers. Call and ask questions about the quality of the work the person did.

- Trust your feelings. Don't hire someone who makes you uncomfortable.

Going to Court

Last spring, Jack hired a carpenter to do some repairs. The carpenter worked for a few days but didn't finish the job. Jack kept calling him to ask about the work. His calls went unanswered. He left messages but never got a call back. What can Jack do?

Many people with problems like this go to small claims court. This is a type of state court that handles disagreements involving small amounts of money. Every state has different limits, up to $10,000. Each person in the disagreement presents his or her side of the issue. Attorneys aren't needed. A judge listens to each person's story. Then a decision is made.

Consumer Protection Agencies

Every state has a consumer protection agency or office of consumer affairs. The U.S. government does too. These agencies:

- enforce laws that protect consumers.

- help consumers avoid unfair practices.

- provide licenses for doing certain jobs.

- tell consumers about their rights.

- help settle consumer complaints about poor work or service.

Chapter 4

Bargain Hunting

A bargain is a really good deal. It usually means buying a high-quality item for well below the normal cost. Hunting down a great deal can be a lot of work. But for smart shoppers, finding a bargain makes it all worthwhile.

Learn the Language of Bargain Shopping

Paying a low price doesn't always mean you're getting a bargain. Sometimes, the price is low because the quality is low.

Look for these words to make sure you know what you're buying:

- **"Irregular" or "Flawed":** These words may appear on a label. They mean a product isn't quite perfect. It may have some design imperfections, such as an uneven hem. Depending on what the product is, its appearance may not matter to you.

- **"As is":** This also means the product isn't perfect. There may be a small scratch or stain. An "as is" item of clothing may be missing a button. It might have a torn seam. These products may work just fine but not look the best.

Buying a flawed, irregular, or "as is" item means you accept its less-than-perfect quality. After you buy it, you probably won't be able to return it.

Where can you find bargains on new items? Outlet stores sell well-known brands at greatly reduced prices. These stores are often grouped in areas to form outlet malls.

Finding Used Bargains

Bargain hunters can save a lot of money by shopping for used items. Many used items are in good shape. Even so, make sure to look them over carefully before buying. You usually can't return used items.

Where can you find used items?

Thrift Stores and Consignment Shops

Search online to find stores that sell used items. Look for thrift stores and consignment shops.

- Thrift stores sell used items that people donate. That means they give the items to the store for free. The money thrift stores make often supports a charity. This could be a hospital or a church. Some stores have half-price days or special bargain days.

- Consignment shops often have high-quality used furniture and clothing. Individuals bring in their used items. When the items sell, the individuals get some of the money. The shop keeps the rest. Great bargains can be found at these types of shops.

Tips for Bargain Hunters

- Collect coupons. Keep them organized. Carry paper coupons with you in a small envelope or wallet. There are apps that can help you organize digital coupons.

- Join online groups for bargain shoppers. Look at the offers they send you for local stores and restaurants.

- Find a grocery store that has double-coupon days. Look at your local grocery store's weekly ad to see what's on sale.

- Become a member of a wholesale shopping club. An annual fee is usually required to join.

- Shop at outlet stores. Find nearby outlet stores that sell the brands of products you like.

Classified Ads

You can also find bargains by reading the classified ads. Find these online or in the newspaper. The prices in classified ads aren't always firm. You can often **negotiate**. Some ads may even say "OBO." That stands for "or best offer." This means you can tell the seller what you're willing to pay. If you offer a lower price and the seller accepts, you can save even more money.

Estate Sales, Bazaars, and Benefit Sales

Some classified ads tell about estate sales and bazaars or benefit sales.

- An estate sale sells items from someone's home, often after the owner has passed away. Household items are usually good bargains at estate sales. Furniture is too.

- Bazaars and benefit sales are held to raise money for charities, schools, and other causes. At these sales, people donate crafts, food, and all sorts of used items to be sold at bargain rates.

Garage Sales, Flea Markets, and Swap Meets

Garage sales are good places to find bargains too. They often take place on weekends. Sometimes, many families get together and have a big neighborhood sale.

Flea markets and swap meets are like giant garage sales. They're usually held every weekend in large outdoor areas. These places may be fairgrounds or parking lots. For a fee, you can reserve a space to sell items. Some states also require sellers to have special permits or licenses.

Shopping With Online Classified Ads

Online ads may be posted on websites. These sites are locally based, usually around large cities. Some sites target rural areas. Others offer specific types of items. Craigslist and Facebook Marketplace are two popular online classified sites.

People who use online ads must follow the rules and guidelines of the website. For instance, there may be rules about how many ads one person can put on the site. If you shop at online sites, be careful not to become a victim of fraud. Never share your Social Security or bank account number.

If an item is local, the seller may be willing to drop it off. You may also be able to pick it up. However, many people are uncomfortable giving a stranger their address. To avoid this, suggest meeting the seller in a public place during the day. Police stations are a safe location.

Buying Items at Auctions

At an auction, items are put up for sale. People place bids. The highest bidder wins the item. In other words, the item goes to the person who offers to pay the most for it. Auctions are held online too. For an online auction, people can browse an auction website and look at what items are for sale. If there's something they'd like to buy, they put in a bid. When the auction ends, the seller will make arrangements to send the item to the highest bidder.

Tips for Bidding in Online Auctions

- Read the description of the item you're interested in. Contact the seller with any questions.

- Check the seller's history at the website. Find out whether anyone has complained about him or her.

- Determine the cost of shipping. Some sellers charge extra to make more money.

- Don't bid on something if you don't trust the seller.

- Compare the prices of the same or similar items being sold by other people.

- To top other people's bids, go up pennies at a time.

- Pay for what you buy using a credit card. Don't pay with cash, check, or money order.

- Never give out your Social Security or bank account number.

Shopping for Goods

Not all shopping is buying things for fun. Sometimes, you'll have to purchase household items, such as a refrigerator or mattress. You might also need clothes for work. When you shop for goods like these, try to get the most for your money. To do that, explore your options. Check out both new and used goods. Also look at items available online and in catalogs.

Getting Started

Jamal is excited about his new job. It starts in two weeks. But before he goes to work, Jamal has a lot to do.

Taking the job means moving to a new city. Jamal has already rented an apartment there. It isn't fancy, but he likes it. *Having my own place will be great,* he thinks.

There is just one problem. Jamal doesn't have much to put in his new apartment. He lived with his family until he graduated from high school. After that, he shared a house with some friends. Besides his clothing, all Jamal owns are a bed, a small TV, and some towels.

Jamal's clothing situation isn't great either. Most of his clothes are casual. They won't work for his new office job. He can't afford to buy a whole new **wardrobe**. Still, he will need a few things to get started.

Before deciding what clothes he needs, Jamal looks through what he already owns. There are a few things he could wear to work. Jamal browses his favorite clothing store websites. Then he orders some nice pants and shirts. He chooses basic styles and colors. They will be easy to match with other clothes—now and later.

Next, Jamal makes a list of the household goods he needs. He knows he can get some of them from his family. His parents have old furniture in the basement, including a dresser, a table, and some chairs. Jamal wouldn't have picked out these things to buy at a store. But knowing what furniture costs, he is happy to have these used pieces. They will get him started in his new home.

Chapter 1

Buying Household Goods

Imagine moving into your own apartment. When you walk through the door, you see empty rooms and bare walls. Now it's time to furnish the rooms. You probably can't afford to buy everything all at once. So, where do you start?

List Your Needs

First, make a list of the things you need most. Begin with basic furniture. This includes a bed, a table, and chairs. Next, list small household items, such as pots and pans, towels, and sheets.

Then, consider household appliances. Will you need to buy a TV? What about a toaster or a microwave?

Set Your Priorities

After you've made your list, decide which items you need right away. Label those items with a number 1. Then label the other items in order of their importance—2, 3, 4, and so on.

The items labeled 1 are your top priorities. A bed, for example, is more important than a bookshelf. Once you've set your priorities, you'll know what to buy now and what to get later.

New or Used?

Think about how to save money on your top-priority items. Also think about which items to buy new versus used. Use these tips to help you decide:

- Buying used furniture will save a lot of money. Check classified ads, estate sales, garage sales, and flea markets.

- For health reasons, it's best to purchase a brand-new mattress. But look for a used box spring and bed frame.

- Many household items, such as pots and pans, can also be purchased used. Look for them at thrift stores, estate sales, and garage sales.

- Your family and friends may have household items they don't use. To help you get started, they might give these items to you or sell them for very little.

Thrift Stores

Are you looking for bargains on household items? A good place to start is your local thrift store. People donate household goods and clothing to thrift stores. These items are then sold at bargain prices. If you're lucky, you can sometimes find new items or older items that were never used and are still in excellent condition.

Chapter 2

Assembling a Wardrobe

Your lifestyle determines the kind of wardrobe you need. Think about your usual activities. The clothes you wear most often should be your first priority. Next, think about what you do the rest of the time. Clothes for these activities should be your second priority.

For example, Leo is a student with a part-time job. He needs clothes for fun, work, and school. What kind of clothes should Leo make his priority?

Tips for Building a Wardrobe

- Make a list of what you need before you shop for clothes.

- Stick to your priorities. Otherwise, you may waste money on things you don't really need.

- Buy good-quality clothes that will last. A few well-made pieces are better than lots of clothes that will wear out fast.

- Choose basic styles you can make formal or informal for different activities.

- Avoid paying a lot of money for trendy clothes. These will soon go out of style.

- Choose new clothes that go with clothes you already have. Try to create several new outfits from each new item you buy.

- Buy clothes for comfort and fit. You won't want to wear clothes that are too big or small.

- Read the fabric labels of clothes before you buy them. Check to see what kind of cleaning and care they will need. Avoid buying clothes that wrinkle easily or have to be dry cleaned. Some dry-clean-only clothes can be washed by hand.

- Remove clothing stains right away. If left untreated, they can become permanent.

- Change into old clothes for play, housework, and messy jobs. Wear an apron when cooking.

- Shop for clothes at discount stores and outlets.

How to Recognize Good Quality

- **Cloth:** Look for fabric that flows and drapes nicely. Also check for even color and weaving. Patterns, such as stripes and plaids, should line up.

- **Seams:** Turn the garment inside out. Look at the seams. This is where the pieces are sewn together. Check for straight, tight seams. There shouldn't be any loose threads. Make sure the ends of seams are secure.

- **Closures:** Zippers, buttons, and other fasteners should be secure. Check that they work properly.

- **Fit:** Try on the item. Does it hang and fit well? Are the coloring and style right for you?

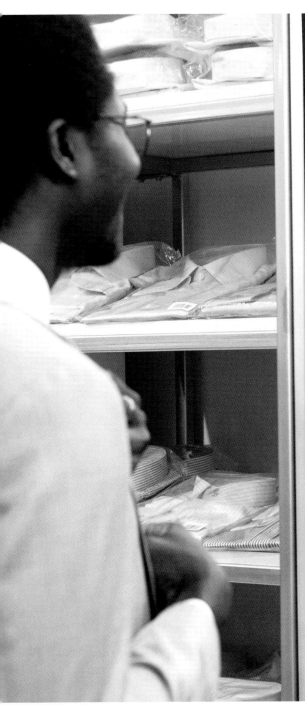

Smart Buys in Clothing

What items of clothing are worth spending more on to get good quality?

- shoes, belts, and handbags in neutral colors; these can be mixed and matched

- clothes you can dress up or down (e.g., plain black pants or a basic black dress)

- classic styles, fabrics, and colors that will stay in fashion

- clothes that fit well and flatter you

- items you will wear often

Tips for Clothing Care

- Wash clothes only when necessary.

- Follow the care instructions on clothing labels.

- Hang items on a line to dry.

- Iron only if needed.

- Hang clothes on good-quality hangers in an uncrowded space.

- Fix tears, ripped seams, and loose buttons. Do this right away, before they get worse.

- Treat stains with stain or spot remover. Then wash the item immediately in cold water. Repeat if necessary. Hot water and hot dryers can set a stain. This means it becomes permanent.

Chapter 3

Shopping From Home

Few things are as convenient as shopping online. Today, most stores and brands have websites where you can shop.

Advantages of Shopping From Home

- It is easy to shop whenever you want, day or night. You don't need to worry about traffic, crowds, or waiting in line for service.

- You can find nearly anything you want, new or used. Plus, you can get things from marketplaces all around the world.

- Many online stores have great prices. This is especially true if you buy direct from a factory or a discount warehouse.

Why Shop Online?

In the U.S., online retail sales are growing. They're expected to reach $1 trillion by 2023.

Why do people like to shop online?

- Checking prices at multiple retailers is quick and easy.

- Information about product features is readily available.

- Online retailers can usually tell you if they have an item in stock.

- In some cases, shipping is free.

Disadvantages of Shopping From Home

- Because it's so convenient, you may buy more things than you need or can afford.

- Shipping fees can be high. This depends on what you buy, where it ships from, and how soon you want it. To save money, look for retailers that offer free shipping.

- Descriptions, pictures, and reviews are all you have to go on before making a purchase. You can't actually inspect or try on what you're buying until it arrives.

- Returning items can be difficult. If you're unhappy with what you buy, you'll often have to ship it back. That means paying a return shipping fee. Some companies also charge a restocking fee. This is a charge for putting returned items back on the shelves. Carefully consider doing business with companies that charge this kind of fee.

- It's easy to spend a lot of time shopping online.

- Some companies use a large amount of packaging materials when shipping items. If you've ordered multiple items from the same place, see if they can be sent together in the same box. Shipping may take a little longer, but less packaging will be used. You might also save on shipping costs. In any case, recycle as much of the packaging material as possible.

Placing an Order

- Keep records of all the orders you place. When shopping online, receipts will be emailed to you.

- Look for discount codes. Sometimes these will be shown right on a retailer's website. Enter the codes at checkout. You can also join the retailer's email and text message lists. Then you'll be the first to know about special offers and sales.

- See what options are available for shipping. Usually, the faster the shipping method, the more it costs. Also check whether free shipping is available.

- Deal only with well-known stores and websites that have good return policies. If you have questions about a store's **policy**, reach out to the retailer. You can find contact information on their website. Some sites also offer a chat option. This lets you speak with someone online while you shop.

Tips for Safe Online Shopping

- Shop only from online stores you trust. Learn about unfamiliar stores on the Better Business Bureau's website.

- Look for security symbols on the checkout page. These include a closed padlock, the words Secure Sockets Layer (SSL) or Transport Layer Security (TLS), and a URL that begins with "https."

- Check the store's privacy statement. It will tell you how your personal information will be used. If you can't find a privacy statement, don't shop at the store.

- Pay with a credit card. If anything goes wrong with your purchase, you'll be protected.

- Save or print out all records of your purchases.

- Many online retailers require you to create an account. When you do, pick a login and password carefully. Choose a password that you'll remember but that no one else will guess.

Chapter 4

Return Policies

Most stores will let you return something that's **defective**. When you return something that doesn't work, you may have three choices:

1. **Exchange:** You can exchange the item for another one.

2. **Store credit:** You can get a store gift card equal to the amount you spent on the item you're returning. The gift card can be used to purchase something in the store that same day, at a later date, or from the store's website.

3. **Refund:** You can get your money back. If you originally paid with cash, you'll get cash back. Otherwise, the refund will be applied to your debit or credit card.

Often, purchased items work just fine. Still, you might decide you don't want what you bought. You may end up not liking the color or size. Most of the time, it's okay to change your mind. Unused items with sales tags or accompanied by a receipt can usually be exchanged or returned.

Making Illegal Returns

Returning items under false conditions is a type of theft. This crime is committed by:

- stealing something from a store and then returning it for money without a receipt.

- paying for something using a stolen check or credit card and then returning the item for cash.

- buying an item and planning to return it after using it.

- changing the receipt to make the price higher and then returning the item for a refund.

Guidelines for Making Returns

You can usually return something you don't want. But you should follow these guidelines:

- Don't wait too long after purchasing an item to return it. Most stores have policies that say how long you have to make a return. This is often 30, 60, or 90 days, but every store is different.

- Make sure you bring the receipt. This proves that you purchased the item. Having the receipt is the key to a problem-free return.

- Bring the original packaging or box. Also bring the sales tag, instructions, and all other materials that came with the item.

- Return the item to the customer service department at the store where you made the purchase. Some chain stores let customers return items at any of their branches. Check their policy first, though. Not all stores offer this convenience.

- If you paid with a debit or credit card, bring it with you. The store may need your card to exchange or refund the purchase.

Return Policies Vary

Before you buy, know the store's return policy. Stores usually post their policies where you can see them. This might be near the cash register. Sometimes it's on the back of your receipt. You can also check online.

Here are some examples of return policies and what they mean:

- **"A complete refund for any reason."** You'll almost certainly get your money back.

- **"Returns only in exchange for other merchandise."** The store will give you a store credit or exchange the item for another one of the same price. You won't get your money back.

- **"No returns of any kind."** Stores that sell used or discounted items usually have a "no returns" policy. You'll be stuck with anything you buy.

Nonreturnable Items

There are some items that most stores refuse to allow customers to return. These may include:

- **Food and other perishables:** An exception might be a perishable item that was already spoiled when you purchased it.

- **Items purchased for big discounts:** This includes sale items that are marked "as is," "all sales final," or "no returns."

- **Used items:** Stores can't resell these items. That means many won't take them back.

- **Personal items:** Things like underwear and makeup can't be returned because of health reasons.

How Returns Drive Up Prices

Stores lose money when they take back merchandise. A large store or chain of stores can lose millions of dollars a year by accepting returned items. In the U.S., the cost of illegal returns is around $18 billion a year.

To make up for these losses, stores often raise their prices. Store managers look at sales records to determine how much money is lost to returns. They figure out what percentage of earnings is lost every year. Then they raise prices to cover that loss. Of course, consumers pay the extra cost.

Shopping for Services

Another kind of shopping involves buying services. These can include things such as insurance, TV and internet, and home repair work. Paying for these services can be expensive. Sometimes, you make monthly payments for years. Other times, you pay up front for work that you expect to last a long time. Spend your money wisely. Be sure to shop around for professional services. Try to find the best quality and the most competitive price available.

Making Smart Decisions

Maria and her husband, Dave, are so excited. They have just bought a house. For years, they cut expenses and saved money. Today at the bank, they signed countless documents. After they finished, the house was theirs.

The couple has many ideas for fixing the place up. It needs some work, for sure. They plan on doing certain things themselves. Maria will paint the bedrooms. Dave wants to fix up the yard. For other projects, they will need to hire professionals.

One of their planned projects is **remodeling** the bathroom. Maria and Dave will speak with several **contractors** about doing the work. Maria thinks they should get different opinions of the time and cost needed for the project. Then they can decide which service provider to hire.

Dave talks to the local cable TV company about setting up service. He is surprised to learn that they can get TV, telephone, and internet service all from the same company. This will save them money. The house has never been wired for cable TV. That means some extra work will be needed. But Dave and Maria are new customers. They will get some of this work done for free.

Still, Maria isn't sure if they need telephone and TV service. She and Dave only use their cell phones. Neither of them watch much TV either. Just using a streaming service is likely a good choice for them. That will let them watch movies and TV shows. But it will be less expensive than cable. All they need is an internet connection. Dave agrees that getting internet service only is the best decision for now.

Something else Maria and Dave plan to check into is insurance. They already have car insurance. To buy the house, they had to get homeowners insurance too. Life insurance is also on their list. Protecting the things they have worked hard for is important to them.

Chapter 1

Checking Reputations and References

From time to time, everyone needs the help of a professional service provider to take care of a problem. A professional is someone who has training and experience in a particular kind of work.  Examples include carpenters, plumbers, and electricians. Tailors, seamstresses, and lawn care workers are professionals too.

Choose a Professional Service

How should you choose a professional service provider? Shop around, just like you'd shop for anything else. First, consider your needs. Then, look for people who can do the job right. Finally, compare prices.

Professional service providers who do repair work must pass state tests and be licensed. If a service provider is licensed, the license number is often shown in ads or on the company's website. Having a license doesn't prove that a service provider is honest. It doesn't mean you'll get the best prices either. But a license does usually mean that the company's workers are experienced, and you'll be protected if something goes wrong.

Get Referrals and References

Many professionals who do repairs are known for doing good work at honest prices. They have a good **reputation**. How can you find these service providers?

Ask family members, friends, and anyone else you trust for **referrals**. Who have they hired that they would recommend? Also ask who they would not recommend, based on their experiences. You can find reviews for service providers online too.

Contact the service providers that others have recommended to you. Ask what they charge. Find out when they're available to work. Also ask each provider for three references. Call those people and ask about the quality of work the service provider did for them.

Is a Professional Service Provider Licensed?

There are two main benefits to hiring a service provider that is licensed:

1. Workers can be trusted to have the skills, knowledge, and experience needed to do a good job.

2. You will likely be protected if something goes wrong. This is because service providers usually need to show proof of insurance when getting a license. In most states, this is required.

Before you hire a service provider, ask to see their license. Find out what office issued the license, and contact it. Ask these questions:

- Does the service provider have a current license?

- How long has the service provider been licensed?

- Was the license ever taken away? If so, why and for how long?

Get Estimates

Ask each professional service provider for a free written estimate. Each estimate should give you a good idea of the following:

- what work needs to be done

- how long the work will take

- when the work will begin and end

- how much the work and any parts or materials needed for it will cost

Don't rush to hire a service provider. Take the time to ask questions first. Make sure you understand the work that's needed. Never agree to anything that you don't understand, want, or need. Think carefully before making a decision. Then call each professional. Let them know if you will or won't be working with them.

Use Your Best Judgment

Cost isn't everything. Don't hire the professional with the lowest estimate just because it's the lowest. Instead, choose a service provider who:

- takes time to explain the job in a way you understand.

- makes suggestions that could save you money.

- guarantees their work and promises 100% satisfaction or your money back.

- carries accident insurance for the worker who does repairs in your home.

- has been in business a long time and can name satisfied customers.

Questions to Ask References

- Was the job done well, on time, and within budget? If not, why?
- Did workers treat the property and family members with respect?
- How well did workers communicate what needed to be done?
- Did workers clean up after themselves?
- Were there any problems? If so, how were they resolved?

Stay away from any service provider who:

- charges for giving you an estimate.
- offers a very good deal but only if you agree to sign a contract on the spot.
- requires payment up front to buy materials.
- demands payment before the work is finished or asks to be paid in cash.
- won't accept payment with a credit card.

How Much Should Repair Work Cost?

Rates can vary widely among professional service providers. Before you hire a company, consider these guidelines:

- **Qualifications:** The more training and experience workers have, the higher the rate.

- **Basic rate:** Some service providers charge by the hour. Often, the first hour costs more. Other service providers charge a flat fee for a certain kind of job.

- **Insurance:** Insured service providers cost more, but they offer protections if something goes wrong.

- **Scheduling:** Doing a big job or several small jobs at once can cost less per hour than a small job.

- **Parts and materials:** The cost of any parts and materials needed will be added to your bill.

- **Travel:** Many service providers charge for travel time. This charge is often called a trip fee.

Chapter 2

Hiring a Professional Versus Doing It Yourself

Sometimes, it's worth it to hire a professional to perform a service for you. Other times, it pays to do the job yourself.

How do you make this decision? It depends on the work that needs to be done. Your skills matter too. Don't repair something that's beyond your ability. That could waste time and money. You could also easily make the problem worse. Then you'll need to get the problem fixed by a professional. This will cost you even more.

When to Hire a Professional

You should hire a pro, rather than do the job yourself, if:

- making a mistake could lead to a bigger problem.

- you could fall, get an electric shock, or be hurt in some way.

- poisons or toxic materials need to be handled.

What Goes in a Basic Toolbox?

- claw hammer
- utility knife and extra blades
- tape measure (25 feet)
- tape (duct, electrical, plumbing)
- flashlight
- level
- set of pliers, including needle-nose pliers
- wrenches (adjustable, combination set, Allen set)
- screwdrivers (standard and Phillips)
- electric drill and drill bits
- selection of hardware (nails, screws, washers, nuts, bolts)
- safety glasses
- pencils

Chapter 3

Comparing TV and Internet Services

When it comes to TV and internet services, consumers have many options. Think about your wants and needs. Do you need fast internet speeds for work or gaming? What TV shows do you enjoy? Can you wait for new episodes each week or do you prefer to binge-watch full seasons?

Also consider your budget. Some TV and internet services can be pricey. Before signing up for a service plan, do some research. You may be able to **bundle** services to save money. Find the best option for your lifestyle and budget.

Watching TV

Television is a popular form of entertainment. In the U.S., an estimated 121 million households have at least one TV. Options for tuning in are growing. Broadcast channels are free but offer limited choices based on location. Cable television is popular and provides a wider selection. But cable services can be pricey. Both broadcast and cable also feature commercials.

If you opt for cable, you can choose from different channel packages. Often, the more channels you want, the more you pay. There are also special packages for movie and sports channels. Some are quite expensive. New customers might get special deals on upgraded channel packages. This can be tempting. Always find out what the cost will be after the deal has run out. If it's more than you want to pay, remember to cancel the extra packages before the deal period ends.

Streaming Services

Streaming services are another option. These services are subscription-based, which means viewers pay a monthly fee. They can then watch movies and TV shows on demand. All that's needed is a decent internet connection. People can watch on their TVs, computers, and mobile devices. Depending on the package you pay for, there may also be no commercials.

Many streaming services offer whole seasons of popular TV shows. They also have countless movies. Some services create their own original movies and shows. Viewers can't watch these anywhere else. Livestream channels for news and sports are also available.

Streaming services are an affordable alternative to cable TV. However, be sure to research what types of shows and movies each service offers before signing up. Every service has a different selection. Some people choose to sign up for several streaming services. This gives them more choices. But be aware that you may not be able to stream a brand-new show or movie right away.

Accessing the Internet

For many people, having internet access at home has become a necessity. It is needed for school, work, and entertainment. This means you'll likely require fast speeds and a strong connection.

Internet service providers often offer several plans. Basic plans have slower speeds. This is usually okay for people who don't use the internet much. If you play online video games, use streaming services, or make video calls for work, you'll need to upgrade. Research providers in your area to see what's available. Compare plans carefully. Call each company to see if they offer special deals or promotions. These can save you money. Just remember to find out what the plan will cost after the deal ends.

Bundling Services

Ask your cable company about bundled service plans. These provide two or more services, such as TV, internet, and telephone. The price is usually discounted from the cost of buying the services separately. Some cable companies have reduced prices for bundled plans for new customers. But make sure you understand what the long-term cost will be. Also consider your needs. Don't pay for services you don't need. For example, if you have a cell phone, will you ever use a landline telephone? If not, you might not want to pay for this service.

Accessing Wi-Fi

Wi-Fi is a wireless network for computers and mobile devices, such as smartphones and tablets. It allows devices to connect to the internet without cables. Like cell phones, TVs, and radios, Wi-Fi transmits information over radio waves. All that's needed is an internet connection and a Wi-Fi router. Today, Wi-Fi can be found in many public places. Libraries, airports, and coffee shops often have it. You can also set up a Wi-Fi network quickly and easily in your home. Then you can connect your devices wirelessly.

Tips for Safe Wi-Fi Use

Wi-Fi lets you use your mobile devices wherever you want. But this freedom comes with risks. When using Wi-Fi, your personal data could be stolen. How can you protect yourself?

- Create a strong Wi-Fi password so others can't access your network.

- Keep your devices updated with the latest versions of antivirus software.

- Change your computer settings. Set them so you have to select a Wi-Fi network before connecting. Don't let the computer select one for you. Turn off the file-sharing option when using a public network. Also be sure to turn on the firewall. This will stop hackers from getting into your system.

- Never connect to an unknown Wi-Fi network.

- Use a virtual private network (VPN). Using a VPN helps keep your data safe as it travels over the network.

- Don't do online banking or make online purchases on an open (unsecured) network. Sending emails or instant messages over one isn't smart either.

- Never enter an account number or password on a web page that's not secure. Look for "https" in the address bar.

Chapter 4

Insurance Policies

Buying a home is a big **investment**. To protect it, you'll need homeowners insurance. Life insurance is important too. While shopping around for policies, you may want to look into a new car insurance plan as well.

Having insurance is important. But what exactly is it? Essentially, insurance policies protect people from losing money. People buy insurance policies to cover the costs of damage to their property and themselves. Policies can also cover the cost of damages to other people and their property.

Common Types of Insurance

- **Homeowners and renters insurance policies cover the risks of owning or renting a home.** They also protect the objects inside your home against theft or damage. Anyone who is injured on your property is covered too. Often, damage caused by natural disasters is not covered. You'll need to get separate insurance for things like floods, hurricanes, and earthquakes.

- **Car insurance usually includes some forms of liability and property insurance.** Overall, car insurance protects you from the risks of owning and driving a car. It often covers accidents and theft.

- **Life insurance protects you from death-related financial loss.** A policyholder can name a beneficiary. This is someone, such as a spouse or child, who will receive insurance money if the policyholder dies. Expenses, such as funeral costs for the insured, may also be covered.

Policyholders pay a set amount of money each month. In exchange, an insurance company agrees to pay for costly damages when things go wrong. This gives people some peace of mind. They can own expensive items, such as cars and homes. But if their car is stolen or their house burns down, they won't take a huge financial loss. That's because the insurance company steps in to pay.

Paying Premiums

The price you pay for an insurance policy each month is called a premium. Some companies give a discount when you pay for six months at a time. Premiums vary depending on the **coverage** you want and need. Insurance companies also assess **risk**. For example, living in an area with a lot of crime can affect your premium. This is because it increases the chances of you filing a claim. More filed claims result in a company having to pay out more money. That can drive up the cost of your premium.

It's important to pay your insurance premiums on time. Even one missed payment could cause your coverage to **lapse**. If that happens, you might lose your insurance. Then any damage that occurs will not be covered.

Assessing Risk

An insurance company assesses risk when determining your premium. There are three types of risk they look at:

- **Liability risk is the risk you pose to other people.** For example, your dog may bite a neighbor. You might also cause a car accident.

- **Personal risk is risk you face.** Illness, aging, and unemployment all present personal risks.

- **Property risk is risk to your property.** It may be caused by damage or theft. Examples include your car being smashed by a big tree during a storm or a thief stealing your TV.

Deductibles

The full cost of damages is not always covered by insurance. Sometimes a policyholder must first meet their **deductible**. This is an amount of money that must be paid out-of-pocket. For example, imagine a tree fell on your car. There is $3,000 worth of damage. If you have a $500 deductible, you must pay $500 before insurance kicks in and covers the rest. Policies with higher deductibles often have lower premiums. They still offer financial protection, but you'll pay more out of your own pocket if you need to file a claim.

In some cases, your policy might not cover the full costs of damages even after your deductible is met. If this is the case, you'll owe the remaining amount that isn't covered.

Choosing an Insurance Policy

Purchasing an insurance policy is a big decision. Find out what insurance you're required to have. For example, state laws set **minimums** for car insurance. If you have a **mortgage**, you'll likely need to have homeowners insurance. Purchasing life insurance is up to you. However, it's a good idea to have if you have **dependents** or large **debts**. Life insurance will make sure your dependents aren't left without money to cover living expenses. It may also cover debts so your dependents don't have to.

Be sure to shop around. Not all insurance companies will charge the same premiums for the same amounts of coverage. Compare policies with several companies. Aim to get the best coverage you can for the lowest premium. Discounts are often available. Always ask about them. For example, having a security system may lower your premium. You can also get discounts for bundling insurance policies. This means you buy several policies from one company.

Consumer Rights

Not every purchase is a satisfying one, unfortunately. Have you ever bought something that broke down? Perhaps you paid for a service you were unhappy with. Maybe you've even been taken advantage of by a dishonest business. Understanding your rights as a consumer will help you solve problems like these. Knowing about credit card protections and product warranties can further empower you as a consumer.

Knowing What to Do

It was Wednesday. Will didn't have to work. That afternoon, he would make his weekly visit to see Grandma June. She always had lunch ready when he got there. After they ate, she usually had a few chores for him to do. He didn't mind the work. It was nice to spend time with his grandmother.

But when Will arrived that day, lunch wasn't ready. Grandma June was upset. Just an hour earlier, a man had called. He told her he worked at her credit card company. The man had some questions about Grandma June's account. Grandma June hadn't asked for his name or phone number. But he'd gotten a lot of information from her. She'd given him her credit card number and other important details.

Grandma June got off the phone. Right away, she knew she'd made a mistake. She was embarrassed and worried. "I don't know what to do," she told Will.

Thankfully, Will *did* know what to do. He called the real credit card company. He explained what had happened. Sure enough, someone was already buying things with Grandma June's credit card.

The credit card company canceled the card. Grandma June wouldn't be responsible for the charges. That's because the problem had been reported immediately.

Will had heard on the news about elderly people being victims of fraud. But he knew it could happen to anyone. Knowing your rights as a consumer was important at any age.

Chapter 1

Credit Card Benefits

Have you ever tried to rent a car without a credit card? It's nearly impossible. In fact, many businesses require having a credit card on file before they'll perform a service.

Protection for the Business

When a customer uses their credit card, it protects a business. It does this by guaranteeing two things. First, the business will be paid for the service they provide. Second, they'll also get paid for any extra costs involved. For instance, a car rental company wants to make sure it will get paid if a customer damages a car. That is why paying with a credit card is often required.

Protection for You

Paying for things with a credit card can protect you too. Suppose you feel you've been cheated by a business where you bought something. Did you pay with your credit card? If so, the credit card company will help you settle the problem.

First, try to settle the problem with the business. You may need help from a consumer protection agency. In some cases, you might even have to go to court.

Also report the problem to your credit card company immediately. Call and explain exactly what happened. Explain that you plan to dispute paying for the product or service. Follow up your call with a letter to the credit card company.

Report the problem correctly. Then your credit card company won't make you pay the disputed charge. It won't make you pay other fees on the disputed balance either. That includes the **interest**.

Your Credit History

- **Why is credit history important?** Your credit history is like a report card of how well you pay your bills. Banks and other lenders look at it. It helps them decide whether to lend you money. If you've never had a credit card or borrowed money, you won't have a credit history. That means banks probably won't lend you money.

- **How can you build a good credit history?** Start by getting a credit card. Use it responsibly. Don't spend more than what you can pay back each month. Make all of your payments on time. Also pay your other bills on time and in full as often as possible. If you've never had credit, making payments on time for one year will get you off to a good start.

Other Benefits of Credit Card Use

Using a credit card has other benefits too. Keep in mind that some are clearly better than others:

- **Cash advances:** Most credit cards let you get cash from a bank or **ATM**. Be aware, however, that this kind of loan is very expensive. You'll be charged high interest, plus other fees. But in an emergency, having a quick way to get cash can be very helpful.

- **Cash back:** Some credit cards offer cash back on purchases you make with the card. This is usually a small percentage of the price. Often, this money can be put toward your balance. You may also be able to have the money deposited into your bank account.

- **Extended warranties:** Many products have a warranty. That means the **manufacturer** guarantees the product will work and last for a certain time. Some credit card companies offer to lengthen the time of the warranty if you make the purchase with their card.

- **Lost card coverage:** If your credit card is lost or stolen, call your credit card company immediately. Under U.S. law, if you report the loss before the card is used, you won't have to pay any unauthorized charges. What happens if you report your lost card after it is used? At most, you'll have to pay $50 of the charges.

Costs of Using Credit Cards

When you use a credit card, you're borrowing money. But borrowing money isn't free. Here are costs that come with using a credit card:

- **Annual percentage rate (APR):** The APR is the interest charged on your balance. Your balance is the total amount you owe. Some credit cards don't charge interest for the first few months, if you pay on time.

- **Fees:** Fees are often charged when making a late payment. Expect a fee for getting a cash advance too. This is when you use your card to take out cash. There are also fees for going over the spending limit that's been set for you. Some cards also charge an annual fee.

Remember: You can avoid many fees by paying your bill on time and in full.

Debit Cards Versus Credit Cards

	Debit Card	Credit Card
Whose money am I spending?	Yours. You can't spend more than you have in your checking account.	Someone else's. You're borrowing money that you'll have to pay back.
Can I get this kind of card?	Most people can open a checking account and get a debit card.	You must have a fairly good credit history to get a credit card.
What's my spending limit?	The amount of money in your checking account. Some debit cards have a daily limit.	The amount is set by the credit card company based on your credit history. There's usually no daily limit.
Can I make cash withdrawals?	Yes. You can go to the bank or use an ATM. There may be a fee, and you may have a daily withdrawal limit.	Yes. You can go to the bank or use an ATM. Know that like any other credit card transaction, you will need to repay this money. You'll be charged a high fee and a high interest rate too.

Chapter 2

Making Complaints

You should be satisfied with the goods and services you buy. As a consumer, the law gives you this right. That's why you should always make a complaint if something goes wrong. You're legally entitled to a solution to the problem.

How to Make a Complaint

Most businesses will do their best to settle consumers' problems. If they don't, consumer protection agencies can help people get results.

If you have a consumer complaint, follow these steps to solve it:

1. **Explain the problem.** Be ready to explain what went wrong and why. Make a list of all the events that led up to the problem. Also list any other issues the problem has created.

2. **Decide how you'd like the problem to be solved.** Can the item be exchanged? Are you able to get your money back? Could the work be redone? You get to decide on an acceptable solution. It's your money.

Top Ten Areas of Consumer Complaints

1. **Cars:** dishonesty by sellers; faulty repairs; leasing, rental, and towing disputes

2. **Home Improvement/Construction:** poor-quality work, failure to start or finish a job, lack of required licenses

3. **Retail Sales:** misleading methods such as false advertising; faulty products; delivery issues; problems with rebates, gift cards, and coupons

4. **Landlords/Tenants:** failure to provide services or make repairs, failure to pay rent and other fees, unhealthy and unsafe conditions, illegal eviction practices

5. **Credit/Debt:** disagreements over billing and fees, problems with home loans, improper or illegal debt collection methods, unfair lending practices

6. **(tie) Communications:** confusing offers, problems with installation and service, billing issues with internet and telephone services

6. **(tie) Services:** poor-quality work, false advertising, lack of required licenses

7. **Health Products and Services:** misleading information, failure to deliver products, unlicensed workers, problems with billing

8. **Utilities (cable, gas, electric, and water):** problems with service, disputes over billing

9. **(tie) Fraud:** fake lotteries and sweepstakes, work-from-home schemes, check scams, identity theft

9. **(tie) Household Goods:** misleading descriptions, failure to deliver, faulty repairs

10. **Internet Sales:** misleading practices, failure to deliver purchases made online

3. **Gather your records.** You'll need receipts, bills, canceled checks, estimates, and other records that back up your complaint. In some situations, you may want to take photographs. Make copies of all your records. Never give anyone the originals.

4. **Figure out what action to take.** If you bought a faulty product, take it back to the store. Ask for a refund or exchange. You can also make a complaint to the manufacturer. Are you unhappy with a service you paid for? Call the manager of the business. Explain what you want done. Sometimes, making a phone call can lead to a satisfactory solution.

5. **Write a letter of complaint.** If you can't settle your complaint with a phone call or a visit, write a polite but firm letter. Your letter should do these things:

- Describe the problem. If it's a faulty product, list the date of purchase and the brand and serial or model number. Then say what's wrong with the product. For a faulty service, describe the job and name the person who performed it. Give the date and explain what happened.

- Tell what you've done so far to solve the problem and what solution you'll accept.

- Give a deadline for a reply—for example, ten business days. Explain that if you don't have an answer by then, you'll get help from someone else.

"Lemon Laws"

Many states have special laws to protect consumers who buy "lemons." A "lemon" is a car that keeps breaking down, even after many repairs. In some states, the term applies if a car spends 30 days or more in the repair shop during its first year. Keep records of all repairs that are made. Also take notes during conversations about the repairs.

To know your rights, look up your state's "lemon law." If you suspect you have a lemon, take action. Write a letter of complaint to the dealership where you bought the car. Outline your claim and say how you'd like the company to make things right. Generally, the dealer can choose whether to repair or replace the car. Your claim may also be denied. Then you must decide if you want to take legal action.

6. **Get help.** Several organizations provide help to consumers. Find the phone number of your state's consumer protection agency online. Call the office for advice. Ask to speak with someone who can handle your problem. You can also contact your state's Better Business Bureau (BBB). The BBB collects complaints, answers consumer questions, and helps solve buyer/seller disputes.

Better Business Bureau

The Better Business Bureau (BBB) operates in the United States, Mexico, and Canada. Different BBB offices serve different states, provinces, and regions. Search online to locate the BBB that serves you.

You can contact the BBB for either of these reasons:

- **To check on a business:** The BBB reviews businesses. It also takes complaints from consumers. Contact the BBB to learn about the reputation of a specific business. This is a smart thing to do before hiring a professional service provider.

- **To file a complaint:** The BBB helps consumers solve problems with products or services they've purchased. It also gets involved in cases of unfair or misleading advertising.

Chapter 3

Warranties

Always look for a warranty before you buy something expensive. Doing so is especially important if you're buying an electronic device, like a TV or a computer.

Think of a warranty as a promise made to you by the manufacturer or the seller. This guarantees your satisfaction. It also shows that the manufacturer or seller will stand behind the product.

Read the Warranty

Read the warranty carefully. It should provide information about:

- **What the manufacturer or seller will do.** The product might be replaced, or it might be repaired. You may or may not have to pay for the repairs, depending on the warranty.

- **Where to go for repairs.** Many manufacturers have their own repair shops. You may be required to have the repairs done there.

- **What time period is covered.** Once this time period ends, the manufacturer or seller doesn't have to replace or repair the item.

Pay attention to warranties when you comparison shop. Getting a good warranty might be worth paying a little more. This is especially true for a major purchase.

Kinds of Warranties

- **Implied warranties:** The implied warranty is the law. It protects your right as a consumer to expect high-quality goods. This is why, even if you don't have a written warranty, you can still make a complaint if something goes wrong.

- **Express warranties:** An express warranty is a stated guarantee, either written or oral. The written warranty that comes with many products is an express warranty.

- **Full warranties:** To be considered a full warranty, five conditions must be met:

  1. The time period of the implied warranty is not limited.

  2. There is no charge for the warranty service.

  3. If the manufacturer can't repair the product, the consumer can choose between a replacement or a full refund.

  4. Anyone who owns the product during the warranty period can get warranty service. It doesn't apply for just the original owner.

  5. Consumers don't need to do anything except notify the manufacturer of a problem.

- **Limited warranties:** If any of the conditions of a full warranty are not met, then a warranty is considered limited.

- **Extended warranties:** An extended warranty lengthens the period of the original warranty. Usually, you have to buy an extended warranty. It may make sense to buy an extended warranty for an expensive product that's difficult to fix. But you probably don't need to buy one for an inexpensive product. This could be a waste of money. Shop smart. Buy a good-quality product. Then you shouldn't need to repair it for many years to come.

Some experts don't think extended warranties are worth buying. Instead, they recommend setting money aside each month. This can be used to cover the cost of repairs. Some items never need repairs. In this case, when it comes time to replace the item, use the money you've saved to do so.

Appliance Warranties

When you buy a new appliance, such as a refrigerator, it's covered by the manufacturer's warranty. That warranty is usually good for three months to a year.

If you want a longer period of coverage, you can buy an extended warranty. That warranty will be provided by the store you're buying the appliance from. Extended warranty lengths vary. They may be from one to over five years. Prices vary too. Generally, the longer the term, the lower the cost per year of coverage.

While under warranty, the costs of parts and labor for making repairs will likely be covered. Maintenance checks and normal wear-and-tear may also be covered. This may sound like a good deal. But think carefully before paying for an extended warranty. What are the chances that your new appliance will break down within the next few years? Will the cost of repairs justify paying for the extended warranty? Some people think both situations are unlikely.

Your Obligations

Again, read every warranty carefully. Make sure you know what your **obligations** are. Failing to follow certain rules could void the warranty. Here are some examples:

- The manufacturer may require you to use only authorized repair shops. If you go to an unauthorized shop, you'll void the warranty. The same is true if you try to fix the item yourself.

- A warranty might require you to show your receipt before having repairs done. The receipt proves when you bought the item. It's important in figuring out whether the warranty is still in effect. If you don't have the receipt, you won't be protected by the warranty.

- The warranty might include requirements for taking care of the product. For instance, a car warranty might require you to have the oil changed every three months. If a problem results from your lack of care, the warranty will be voided.

Tips for Buying an Extended Car Warranty

1. **Look at what services are provided, not just the price of the warranty.** Try to get a warranty that covers both breakdowns and regular wear-and-tear.

2. **Shop around.** Talk to the dealership where you bought the car. Also look online for companies that sell extended warranties.

3. **Check out the company that's providing the warranty.** Contact the BBB to learn the company's history and reputation.

4. **Look for a warranty that's transferable.** That means it continues to cover the car after the car has been sold to someone else.

5. **If possible, get approval to bring your car into any repair shop.** Also try to get towing service covered.

6. **Try to avoid having a deductible.** With a deductible, you have to pay a certain portion of the cost of the repairs.

Chapter 4

Telephone and Internet Scams

Some of the methods used by **telemarketing** and internet marketing are **legitimate**. But not all of them are honest. A few are even illegal.

Avoid Scams

Telephone and internet **scams** try to trick people out of their money. Millions are scammed each year. Be **cautious** when strangers try to sell you something over the phone or in an email. In particular, look out for people who:

- try to pressure or rush you into buying something.

- say you've won a prize but ask you to pay for shipping to receive it.

- ask you to pay for something in advance.

- claim to be someone you know and ask for money to get out of trouble.

- ask for personal information, such as your Social Security, bank account, or driver's license number.

- tell you to call a long-distance number to enter your name in a sweepstakes.

- refuse to give you their name and phone number.

Protect Yourself

- **Stop the calls:** You can ask telemarketers to stop calling. If the calls continue, speak with your local phone company or consumer protection agency. They can tell you how to take action to stop calls.

- **Block the emails:** You don't have to open every email message you receive. It's best not to open emails from people you don't know. Many computers have programs that prevent the delivery of unwanted messages. Contact your email provider for more information about spam filters.

- **Stop the texts:** If a company sends you text messages, you should be able to opt out of receiving them. Often, you can reply to a text with "STOP" and the company will no longer send you messages.

- **Turn down trial offers:** Some companies use "free trial offers" to sell their products. They may even claim that you have "no risk or obligation." But find out for sure. By accepting a trial offer, you may be agreeing to purchase products or services in the future. After the trial period runs out, you may get billed for a monthly subscription. If you accept a trial offer, cancel the agreement after you've received the free products. Otherwise, you might get billed for additional items. You may also get charged for shipping and other fees.

Sign Up for the "Do Not Call" List

A law was passed in 2007 that gives Americans the right to stop calls from telemarketers. You can stop getting these calls by signing up on the Do Not Call Registry. You can do this online or by phone. Once you sign up, the calls should stop within 31 days. Telemarketers that continue to call can be fined by the U.S. government.

How to Stop Getting Unwanted Email

There is an easy way to stop getting unwanted emails. Just set up your computer to block or delete these messages. Look for settings that control "junk mail" or "spam." These settings are sometimes called "email rules."

You can also stop getting email from specific companies. To do that, open one of these emails. Scroll down to the bottom of the message. Look for a link that lets you "unsubscribe." Click on it. Then enter your email address and click the "unsubscribe" button.

Smart Consumer Dos and Don'ts

- **Do compare the prices at regular stores with the prices in online offers.** Remember that buying at a regular store means you don't have to pay for shipping.

- **Do use common sense.** Things that sound too good to be true usually are.

- **Do take the time to understand every offer and talk it over with someone you trust.**

- **Don't do business with a company that uses only a P.O. box for an address.** If you have a complaint, you may have trouble contacting the company.

- **Don't give out personal information just because someone asks you for it.** Refusing to answer personal questions isn't being rude. It's being smart and safe.

- **Don't send money or give someone your credit card or bank account number to get a free prize, product, or service.**

Common Scams to Watch Out For

- **Phishing:** Email scams in which people are tricked into giving out their personal information. Examples include the numbers and passwords to bank accounts or credit cards.

- **Vishing:** Phone scams in which callers pretend to be financial service workers. They try to trick people into giving them personal information and account numbers.

- **Smishing:** Text message scams in which senders try to get people to click links that go to bad websites. Then they collect personal information.

Be a Savvy Spender

Spending money is easy. Everyone has items they have to buy and services they need to pay for. But how can you know if you're spending your hard-earned money wisely? Be aware of tricks used in advertisements, understand your wants versus your needs, and look into the reputation of a service provider before hiring someone for a job. It's also a good idea to understand how credit cards work. Always be on the lookout for potential scams. Being a smart consumer will save you money and prevent frustration.

GLOSSARY

ATM: stands for automated teller machine; a machine used to take cash out of a bank account

authorize: to give someone permission

bundle: to group products or services so they are sold together

cautious: mindful of risk or danger

clause: a stand-alone part of a legal document

consumer protection agency: an organization that upholds the rights of people who make purchases

contract: a written agreement that is bound by law

contractor: someone hired to do work within a certain time frame for a specified price

coverage: financial assistance provided by an insurance policy

debt: money that is owed to another person or business

deductible: the amount of money someone must pay to fix something before their insurance company will begin to cover the rest of the cost

defective: having a problem that keeps something from working properly

dependent: a person, such as a child, whose basic necessities must be provided for by another person

entitle: to give someone the right to something

fraud: a crime where someone falsely represents themselves in order to steal from another person or organization

interest: a percentage paid to someone for the use of their money

investment: money that is spent now to buy into something that is likely to grow in value

lapse: to stop being valid

legitimate: real or accepted

license: a document that gives a person the right to do something

manufacturer: a company that makes something

minimum: the least or smallest amount that is possible or allowed

mortgage: a legal agreement to pay for a house or property over a period of time

necessity: something you must do or have

negotiate: to formally discuss something in order to come to an agreement

obligation: something you have to do because of a rule, law, or promise

perishable: likely to spoil quickly

permit: an official document that allows a person to do something

policy: a document that contains an agreed upon set of rules

promotion: advertising that is done to increase awareness of a product

referral: the act of sending someone to a different business for help

remodel: to change the shape, structure, or appearance of something

reputation: what many people think about someone or something

risk: a chance that something bad will happen

scam: a way to get people's money by lying to them

telemarketing: the job of selling services or goods over the telephone

toxic: poisonous; harmful

void: to make something invalid

wardrobe: a collection of clothing

warranty: a promise a company makes that an item will work; the company will repair or replace the item if it stops working during a stated period of time after it was purchased

LIFE SKILLS HANDBOOKS

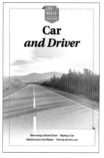

9781680219821

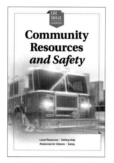

9781680219913

9781680219838

9781680219845

9781680219852

9781680219869

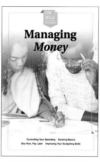

9781680219883

9781680219890

9781680219906

9781680219876

For more information, visit:
www.sdlback.com/life-skills-handbooks